LOST & FOUND

POEMS OF LIFE AND LOVE

LOST & FOUND

POEMS OF LIFE AND LOVE

LYN BEYER

IRON HORSE

IRON HORSE ENTERPRISES, LLC
Leawood, KS

IRON HORSE

First Edition: December 2015

ISBN: 978-0692594933

10 9 8 7 6 5 4 3 2 1

CONTENTS

INTRODUCTION

Over forty years ago, I promised myself that I would publish my poetry. That day has finally come. But time, experience and perspective have altered the reasons. It is now important that I share my thoughts with others who may feel the same emotions but are unable to express them. Time has shown me that the feelings I put to paper have no beginning or end but are eternal in the human psyche.

My hope would be that I may reach emotions and feelings that my readers have tucked away too long. Experiences in relationships that were happy and memorable or filled with pain. Hope is eternal—so relax and allow your emotions to drift and carry you away. These are familiar feelings that I hope fit you like a glove.

I was fortunate to have a muse. Several, actually. And I dedicate this collage to them. This flight of my imagination has kept me in my youth to this very day. Never give up and never stop dreaming.

- Lyn Beyer

FOR TOMORROW

We spent ourselves with one another
Last night. We were just being honest.
No guilt; no shame; no tomorrow!
One night—one lifetime. Sometimes
There is so little difference. I'd like
To say it doesn't matter that you
Left before I woke—but it does—
I heard you leave and I cried a
Tear for a love I hoped would be.
When I was small I liked to
Pretend, but not anymore. Not
With you. There have been too many
Transients in my life. I thought
You were different somehow. And so
I gave myself to you yesterday—hoping
For tomorrow.

THE VERY THOUGHT

The very thought I have of you,
And those I always will,
Are happy, joyful, carefree ones
That linger with me still.

I cannot judge your beauty
By any I have known,
And I'll dream of you, my Dearest;
Long to call you, "all my own."

But like a flower at winter time
That withers and must die,
Your love for me is crushed, and lo
A beggar once more am I.

COMINGS AND GOINGS

With all the comings and goings in our lives;
All the people, all the places.
It's the people that leave the impressions.
Some just bounce off our armor—
Some may even dent it.
But that one special someone
Can come out of nowhere
And pierce your heart.
Through your defenses,
Through your armor.
God blessed me with you—
From the first smile—
    You had me.
My armor pierced, my heart
    Captured
By your very presence.

LOVE CHANGES

Love changes, you know.
It ebbs and flows much like
    The tide.
It washes over you and
    Washes away.
But it's still love—and it
    Changes.
Love is different on a misty
    Night under a street lamp
Than on a day filled with
    Sunshine.
It's different in the winter
    While cuddling on a couch
Than in the spring when
    Flowers bloom.
You always helped me through
    The changes;
Changes that seemed like
    Hurdles to me were just
    A smile for you.
God, I love you.

THE OTHER DAY

We spoke the other day
And I saw the smile
   That wasn't there.
I saw the flicker of hope
   In your eyes.
I noticed the defensive shell
   From past relationships.
It will take more than words
To crack this shell;
Created by a past love that was
   Fleeting and hurtful.
But I won't let you live
   In the past.
I can't.
I love you too much.
I have the water to nurture
   A withered flower.
Loneliness cannot exist in the
Presence of true love.
The love I hold in my heart
   For you.

CLOUDS

The clouds roll in.
I have watched them from my bedroom window
　　For several hours.
Mesmerized by the coming storm.
You did that to me the first time we met.
Held me in your spell.
Kept me there.
You became a storm in my heart and mind.
And you never left …
You rolled into my life
　　Like those clouds.
Covered my life, my very soul with them.
And you never left …
You had the power to change them
　　From dark to light,
　　From blue to red,
My emotions running wild,
And you never left …
The journey of our love is amazing.
And you never left …

LAST NIGHT

I awoke last night and watched
You for a time in your slumber. The
Moon danced on your naked body
Beside me. And I imagined us
Lovers once again. Maybe we've been
Too long together. Perhaps, we must
Go back to recapture the feelings
That made us one. It is worth
A try, isn't it? How we used to
Curl up on a couch; or lay in the
Cool summer grass and watch the
Stars; and make love. I hope you
Watch me in my sleep and feel as
I do tonight. For if you do, our
Love will last.

I WALKED ALONE

I walked the beach
    We used to walk.
The memories flooded back over me
    Like the tide upon the shore.
I noticed how I couldn't get lost
    As all shoe soles leave a
    Different impression in the sand.
Purpose also makes a difference.
People with a destination leave
    Deep footprints.
Those who walk the beach to
    Commune with nature leave
    A shallower footprint.
Those who walk to meditate and
    Look inward, as I did today,
      Leave almost no footprint.
There is a time for all footprints.
Those with purpose and those without.
I suppose it depends on the sentiment
    Of the day.
Whether a walk with the world,
    Or a walk with God.
Memories and God walks seem to be
    My fare these days and the
    Serenity suits me.
It helps the adjustment from "we" to "me".
With the aloneness and emptiness.
The things we used to do;
The places we used to go—I revisit.
One by one—and feel you beside me.

The memories tell me I must.
My mind tells me it's not the same.
But I search the hollowness of it all
    Just the same.
I know there are things that must be
Important—but I haven't found them yet.
    Maybe someday—somewhere.

MOMENTS

Many wondrous moments
Are made from simple things.
A smile, a walk, a loving touch,
The joys that living bring.

And in these wondrous moments
That rest in silent hours;
I think of you, my Darling,
As rain upon the flowers.

You help them grow and blossom
From leaf to bud and then;
You hurl your rays of sunlight
So they may bloom again.

MY DEAREST ONE

My Dearest One, My Dearest One,
I see you every night;
My eyes behold your beauty
Your eyes are shining bright.
Your virtue and austerity,
Your highborn grace and style,
They put my mind at journey
It wanders many miles.
I see you dance a winning waltz
They've handed you the crown,
I see you wake each morning
Your hair all tumbled down.
I see you on my ceiling
As I lay awake each night,
I see you dressed in fancy lace
That's made from satin white.
To be with you and by your side
To feel the warmth and glow,
That you'd impart to me my dear
This only would I know:
Together we will always be
Till death—eternity.

DREAM LOVE

Of you I dream when once asleep;
And in the arms of slumber do love
You and caress tenderly your lips,
Your neck, your swelling breasts.
To hold you close and feel your
Pulsating heart—hear the panting
Breath of love. And to fondle you
With delicate fingers—a soft warm
Body known to my sense of touch.
And I love and care for your every
Wish and desire because, my Darling,
You are precious; you are mine.
But alas, I wake and find, tis only
The fantasy of an unconscious mind;
And wish you were here or I
Asleep once more.

14

ONLY TO COME AGAIN

I hate the stone upon the beach,
And so I hurl it into the water—
Violently! But to what avail, when
I know that it will only be
Washed back upon the beach again.
Perhaps for a moment, as I cradle
The stone in my palm, I'll call it
Beautiful and cherish it. But only
For that moment. Then once more
I'll hate it, and hurl it into the
Water and bury a memory. Because
I am afraid—afraid that it will
Destroy me! The rock ... the memory?
I do not need that stone, yet I
Depend upon its returning for my very
Existence, and I wait.
I know it will come again, just as
The pain of love—gone now but only
To come again.

LOVE AND I

Love is missed when away—after being
Surrounded by its sheltering warmth
For ever so long.
She's the song I wake up to.
She's the melody I take to bed each night.
Love is even the warm glow on my
Distant face when I recall the night's dream.
Dreams of Love and I together—laughing,
Giggling, rolling in the summer grass and
Mussing each other's hair ... then a kiss.
Never touching reality—but who bothers
To look for it? Who wants it?
Not Love and I.
Love and I are so much in love,
We're creatures in each other's dreams.
Or didn't she know? Seems odd I haven't
Told her ... when it runs through my mind
Constantly!
I guess I'd better tell her ...
My Love, that is.

A FRIEND

I remember you, how could I forget.
You're the softness that
    Cushioned my fall.
The spark that gave me life again.
The glow that shined through the
    Darkest cloud when I was lost.
I found my way then, and that's not all,
That glow not only found me, but
    Kept me.
It was like being in a spotlight of my own;
The light being that of an angel's eyes ...
    Your eyes.
You gave me something
I never had before—
    A friend.
Someone who takes time to care for the lonely.
Someone who listens to thoughts,
    Really listens.
And I learned to listen also.
It's a good feeling—
    Like kids with cookies.
Why, I can even smile now,
And show my heart to you.
Maybe my glow will find someone, too.
Walking in the night—
    Alone.

IN YOUR EMBRACE

My but you're tender in the night.
Or is it my loving you
    That makes me want to
        Bury my face in your breasts,
        Caress their beauty,
        And run my fingers through
        Your golden hair?
Or is it the fire inside us
    When the length of our bodies
        Entwine?
Whatever love is
    It is ours—
        For the fleeting moment of a lifetime;
        The sudden flare of a shooting star;
        The chiming of the old clock in the
        Town square as it strikes midnight.
All this and more
    As our heartbeats
        Quicken.
Lying here with you
    In our undraped innocence—
        Our kisses growing more frantic,
        And our lives
        Becoming
        One.

How Could I?

How could my alone time interfere with
Our time? The day and evening with you
So wonderful and yet I left you out of my
Despair and loneliness. It was so selfish
Of me. I can only vow that it will never
Happen again. I am either with you or not.
Life is that simple but my emotions are
Not. I do love you with all my heart—my
Very soul. But I left you just the same,
And apologize for feelings I could not
Control but should have shared. They
Belong to us now—not just me. I can
Only ask for forgiveness and
Understanding. Flashbacks seem to
Haunt me and coping is difficult.

PARTING

We parted just this morning,
And still the day has not begun.
Already, I miss her.
I remember the soft things about our
Last moment—the kind that melt all
Defenses and leave a hungry, hollow heart.
Her tender cheek from our last hug;
Her golden hair against my skin,
And then a kiss.
But those eyes—those wide eyes that never
Need words to talk,
Clouded, then reached out for me,
And told me what love meant.
And the teardrops that almost made me stay.
I tell myself the summer will not be too long.
It will be full of busy things.
Yet, I know at best, the days and nights
Will be empty without her.
Filled with thoughts and dreams of her
To drive away the monotony.
    I hope the summer is not too long …
    My heart might break.

FINDING EACH OTHER

It's evening now and I've had all the
People I can take for one day.
Walls of people closing in around me.
I must escape and be alone to sort
Through my thoughts. Come with me.
Enter my quiet time and bathe in it.
I could be alone with you forever.
My life hanging on every word that
Touches your lips.
I can't promise you an exciting time—
Just a chance to know me as I really am.
A chance to let down all barriers between
Two people. A chance to share our
Intimate souls. A time to be honest
With someone other than yourself.
Who knows, we might find harmony
By reading to each other; or by touching.
Let me share with you sunrise in Colorado.
The beauty of mountains at days end.
Or trace a drop of sweat down your
Belly with my tongue. We could take it slow;
And if we find ourselves—
We'll find each other.

THE ONLY PART OF ME

If I could promise to you, Dear,
Eternal love at last;
To never leave your side again
Would you forgive my past?

I feel you would because, my Dear,
I know your loving heart.
For many years, we were as one
Together or apart.

I would do this and so much more
That even you would see;
My love for you will always be
The only part of me.

EACH MOMENT

Each moment that I think of you
Each hour of every day;
I think of all the times we've shared
Here, and along the way.

I cling to all the little things
That you have said and done;
How cute you were, and sad, and gay;
 And how I held you, Hon'.

I dream of all the fields we ran
And all the hills we climbed.
How all our lives we've shared each thrill
However low or high.

And each time that I find myself
Lonely, without love;
I think of you, my Darling wife,
And stars appear above.

While We're Apart

I remember days
When all the tears I could have cried
Could not have quelled the fire in
My heart—
    From missing you.
I could feel love then ...
In my younger, wilder days.
But gone now—so many years—
The pain is now a livable world.
Still, lonely days are not unusual.
Climbing, soaring—
Then crashing to depths the heart
Should never know.
    What was it about you?
It could have been so many things.
Though not wanting to remember ...
I call it love—
Then fall asleep.

THE WIND

Oh but were the wind
   A friend of mine
To follow at my heels
   And whisper in my ear.
To challenge smoke rings
   Bathed in silence;
And rescue me …
   From lonely nights.

AGES AGO

It seems ages ago since we first fell in love.
I found the flowers I gave you pressed
Between the pages of a book. I threw the
Book away for it held no memory of you.
But those once beautiful flowers reminded
Me of our love. So I put them with your
Picture knowing they once captured your
Smile. Of course, they're faded like your
Picture, but still I hold them dear.
In my mind, those flowers will always
Bloom as the love we gave each other.
Oh, there were times when parting was
Close; but we would soon remember ...
And we'd cry and hold each other
Close until the feeling disappeared.
What held us together? Memories, I
Guess; and I suppose they always will.
But what's wrong with that on a cold
Lonely night now that you're no longer
Here? It's more than most people have.
Love is such a difficult word to explain
The longer that you live it. So tonight,
As my heart yearns deeper still, and I
Find myself lost without you; I'll
Clutch your picture and smell the
Flowers and fall in love again.

It's Raining Again

It's raining again ... it helps the night
But hinders the day. The days never
Seem to end when the rain closes the
Door on sunshine.
But those nights—long nights—
So comforting when accompanied
By the sound of soft tapping
Raindrops. With you, my wish is
That the rain never ceases, nor the
Night ever end. Does the racking
Sound of thunder make you squirm
And move a little closer—pressing
Until our heartbeats are one?
I could say I never noticed,
But I'd be lying. At night,
Sailing on a river of raindrops;
And flowing with the rhythmic
Breeze. Listening—to the
Pitter-patter of raindrops—
Or heartbeats?

FEELINGS

We don't have much yet.
We've never mentioned love.
Let's be honest with each other.
People aren't honest with each
Other or themselves very often.
As honest and straightforward as
Children are with each other—
And the world.
Let's take that chance.
Maybe then we won't be afraid anymore.
Perhaps, we can put a name to the
Feelings I think we share.
Let's do that; and then, let's start all over.
Let's see how many miles
We can walk together;
How many dreams we can share.
Let's be seen holding hands.
And be honest with ourselves and
Show the world that there are words—
Simple words—for the feelings we share.
Words like closeness, sharing and
Perhaps in time—Love.
And smile—Yes, let's smile.
And return to the simple pleasures
That we can share while we are still young.
Let's travel to places you've
Been but never seen.
They're just around the corner.
We can walk. And if we get tired
We can always catch a bus back home;

Or to somewhere—as long as we're together.
Oh, the beautiful things are just that
Simple if you let them be.
And as long as we're as honest
As children with each other,
There doesn't have to be any hurt.

WHEN WE WERE YOUNG

There was a time when we were one.
I knew your gentle touch in the night.
Your cold feet and quiet slumber. Your
Every sound. I used to kiss your forehead
As you slept and stroke your silken hair.
But it didn't count because you never
Knew it. But I did.
It was my only way of reaching out—
The only moments that mattered.
Our only closeness as time has
Lead me to believe. So many years
Of caring sifted down into such
Precious few moments. But we were
Young—and we were one—
So many years ago.

THE BEACH

I have yet to run beside you down the beach.
To hold your hand in mine
And watch the wind defile your hair.
To kiss away the salt upon your lips,
And kneel beside you; shade you from the sun.

I have yet to follow footsteps in the sand
Knowing that they lead to you.
And to the depths I know exist
In your wild soul
And in wild seas.

I have yet to feel the warmth of sunlight
As it radiates from your body when we touch.
Or frolic at the water's edge;
Or revel at the find of driftwood,
Knowing there is beauty undiscovered—waiting.

I have yet to find you, Darling.
And though my dreams are locked away,
Though I cannot see or touch you;
We'll know each other by our heartbeats,
And meet upon a beach—someday.

LOVE IS TIMELESS

She lies there like a porcelain china doll
Head turned to one side
As if the neck were broken.
But so peaceful in her slumber
    The moon gleaming on her face
    Bouncing off her body
Her curves, her angles, her softness.
There for my eyes only. The soft
Muffled breathing attesting to
The comfort and trust that is
    Unspoken between us.
And yet, every other instinct
Between us almost animal like.
To protect—to care for—to nourish.
Bound together by desire and passion
Seldom seen. Words unnecessary.
Time no longer matters.
Not minutes,
Hours or days.
They fold into each other.
    Love is timeless, you know.
        And words unnecessary.

HER FACE

Every time I see her face
A warmth wells up inside;
  It makes me glow
  Just to know
That she'll be by my side.

Each and every time she smiles
Or simply turns my way;
  I know I've felt
  My cold heart melt
My cares just drift away.

Every time she's close to me
I know that we will be;
  Ever closer
  Drawing closer
The way love's meant to be.

BED OF ROSES

Lying on a bed of roses
Petals gently falling 'round.
None can be as soft as you are
Lying here without a sound.

In the night we'll sleep together
In the day we'll playful go.
Roses soft, may well be, Darling
But none can match the love I know.

SOME DISTANT WORLD

In some distant world—
Some distant future—
It will be written that we found each
Other only by chance ... And yet,
We laughed and loved for an
Eternity.
And maybe that this was, in fact, the
Only Heaven that man could ever really
Know or be certain of.
For, we never really know.
All we can know is what we experience.
And it may be found that laughing,
Loving and sharing are the
Ultimate forms of emotion; and that
Heaven is really a state of mind or
Awareness.
So in some distant future, we may
Have the satisfaction of knowing we
Were there—all the time—yet unknowing.
That's why I love you.

THE MIDDLE YEARS

I find myself in the middle
Of my years.
Alone—empty—searching.
Not knowing where today is—
Or yesterday ended—or tomorrow begins.
Until you. You care, feel, sense the
Same inner longings.
I thought I was the only one that felt that way.
Perhaps I've known you in a dream;
Perhaps, another lifetime!
But when I met you yesterday,
I knew we'd been in love before.
I felt your heartbeat in my soul.
I could sense that you felt mine.
The same oneness. That's why we kissed.
Not an exciting adolescent kiss;
But a moving, merging of our souls.
Who said dreams don't come true?
I found you, didn't I? We don't
Have each other all the time; but we
Know where to escape—each other's arms.
Finding each other was critical.
Touching our lips, touched our souls.
Anything less will be vain.

MISSING YOU

Telling you I miss you now
That you are gone is so empty.
The loneliness settles in like
Some thick fog and there's no
Sun to burn it away.
I remember evening walks and
Holding hands. Laughing as
We sat by a fountain with
People all around, but we never
Noticed—we had our own
World.
Wherever we were became our world.
A world together that only we
Inhabited. Being together and
Relying on each other was all
We ever needed.
The seasons mattered not. Whether
Sun or rain, dark or stormy,
Or the quiet snow—we held each
Other and became one in our
World.
And now those precious memories
Drift back to me as close as
Yesterday and as far away and long ago
As forever.

YOUR SMILE

All the houses on the street
Have porch lights, but in the
Evening the houses sit in darkness.
It's not about saving money;
It's about loneliness and
Keeping the world at a distance.
Porch lights are a lot like
    Smiles.
Your smile was beautiful
    And yet,
       You saved it.
When you smiled, the room
    Lit up.
The light was so blinding
The world seemed to melt
And was at your beck and call.
To use it so sparingly was
    Just not fair to the rest
       Of us—
          Waiting.

THE BEACH REVISITED

It's been six months now.
And once again I visit the
   Memories.
The fun times. The carefree times
When we were the only two on earth.
The beach is that place. And so
I collect shards of broken sea shells.
You did all the wading for me as
I wore shoes and socks. You lived
   Barefoot.
I must have boxes of broken sea shells
At home. It's the walk with you that
   Counts.
Then and now.
The sadness settles in and the
Realization of oneness fits more
Like a glove.
Perspective is more focused now.
It's life that's fleeting—not love.
The broken heart will mend in time.
Not yet, perhaps, but in time.
I'll be back and you'll walk
With me once again. I know
That now. I miss you, Darling.

STRANGERS

Summer always seems
    Too long
Till winter comes.
I loved you then
    And I still do.

I shared my space
    With you
As you shared yours
    With me.
And somewhere beneath
    A full moon
    We became one.

Sometimes strangers pass by
    Sometimes staying
        Usually for a moment,
        A day, a week, a month.

And then summer ends
    And I find myself
        Alone.

UNANSWERED

How will I know when to come to you?
Out of the cold shadows of night.
How will I know? How will I know?
It would only take a smile.
Sitting across the room from you day after day.
The silence is maddening. Time and
Waiting have made me weary with despair.
I must talk to you when you pass this
Way again. You must feel it too. As
Sensitive as your beauty leads me to believe
You are—you must feel it too.
How will I know when to come to you?
How will I know? How will I ever know?

At Last

At last, alone and weary, bewildered by
Life's decisions; I reach out. Feeling your
Touch as only someone solitary could.
Knowing love beyond the crumpled
Walls and shattered shells of mere existence.
At last, I come to you. My thoughts,
My heart, my body—yours alone. The
Great chasm of loneliness bridged by longing.
Becoming one—each giving freely.
Touching, clinging, the flood of emotion—
Released—At Last! Our thoughts, our hearts,
Our bodies entwined. The earth of our very
Souls tremble at each embrace. And time
No longer an enemy. But rather, a quiet
Corner in the night for lovers to share.
Our bodies belonging to one another.
The fear of empty lives—
Overshadowed—
At Last.

YOUR LOVING HEART, AT LAST

If I were just to say to you
Together we must be,
Would you accept proposal,
Or would you laugh at me?

Or would you have to sleep on it,
The way that some girls do?
And wake up to reality
Believing it's not true?

How would the thought of lasting love
Affect your memory?
Would you think of loves gone by
Or good times and of me?

Or would your heart dictate to you
A love that is so vast,
That you would have to give to me
Your loving heart, at last!

HEART ACHE

Having you and not being
    With you
My heart aches.
Being near you and not being
    Able to show my love
Hurts even worse.
My heart and mind feel like
    Exploding.
The emotions so powerful
And in our situation I feel so
    Powerless.
Someday, it will not be this way.
It will try our patience.
    Waiting is not my strong suit.
Life is fleeting
And so is love—sometimes.

Two Worlds

As I gaze into your eyes
I see two worlds colliding
In an explosion of emotions
That only happens once in
    A lifetime.
When I take your hand in mine
My pulse quickens.
When our lips meet,
I get dizzy and weak.
This roller coaster of emotions
We are on shows no signs
    Of slowing down.
It's as if you and I were
Placed in time and space to
    Meet and
Begin a new life as one.
Your glow is that of an angel.
    My angel.

RUN FOR THE LIGHT

There are days when memories
Steal your thoughts, and your
Focus drifts to places that your
Heart cannot absorb.
These are the difficult times.
These are your walls—your limits—
   Your desperate times.
And you turn inward, looking
For an escape that is not there.
There are days of hopelessness
But they will lessen in time—
   I am told.
But you are really the only Master
   Of your mind;
And controlling it is not always possible.
And wanting to matters not.
Find the joy in the sadness
   To find the escape.
And run for the light—
   If you are able.

For Elizabeth

I have soared in the clouds with eagles;
I have been to the depths of hell.
And now I'm somewhere in between,
And I've learned my lessons well.

To learn to love and be loved,
To live without fear and hate;
And then when we find the Altar
God will open the Gate.

For beauty lies not on the outside,
But God buries it deep within.
And the love that you show to your neighbor
Will bring you back home again.

And now it is time for your Birthday,
Though it may be without much ado;
My wish is that you find contentment
In life and in all that you do.

TWICE IN A LIFETIME

Your softness in the evening as the sun
    Fades on the horizon;
The touch and feel of your skin;
The moisture on your lips when we kiss.
This, the pinnacle of the day
Does not hold a candle
    To waking beside you in the morning.
Feeling your lips and body respond
    To my kiss from your slumber
Stirs my very soul…
As your body turns and presses
    Against mine with eyes still closed.
There is no other feeling like this on earth.
So here in the arms of love I'll stay—
As long as you'll let me.
To have this feeling come to you
Once in a lifetime is unique.
To find it twice
    Is Heaven.

THE VERY THOUGHT

The very thought I have of you,
And those I always will,
Are happy, joyful, carefree ones
That linger with me still.

I cannot judge your beauty
By any I have known,
And I'll dream of you, my Dearest;
Long to call you, "all my own."

But like a flower at winter time
That withers and must die,
Your love for me is crushed, and lo
A beggar once more am I.

ONCE AGAIN

I long for the day when, once again,
We can be alone—together.
Side by side, touching; our hearts
And minds blending into that something
Eternal and intangible—called love.
Love that was always there but hiding
From ordinary people—waiting for that
Special someone. A soft tender love
Brought about by perfect harmony.
And sharing, sharing always. Thinking
Thoughts undreamed of and turning
The world into fantasy. And with love,
The disappearance of the mask of
Loneliness that shuts life out.
Love letting in the light of years gone by
And years to come ...
Glowing now with new life and
New love.

Quiet Days

Moss laden rocks from drier days
But now the banks are swollen, the
Foliage dances and serenity pervades.
A hideaway for lovers and dreamers
To watch a leaf the current to follow.
To touch life deeply in a long embrace
And hear the sound of nature and it's
Lovers on the bank.
Catching the ecstasy of life and love
In a moment, as the leaf catches on
A rock and then flows down the stream.
And now the pounding and panting that
Reminds us that life flows on
Once again awaiting another moment
Of quiet harmony—Someday. Maybe
Other lovers will know this moment
As the leaf rests upon a rock once more.
But only for a moment.

Consumed by You

I would find it hard to believe
That the whole world does not smile
When you do. For you have touched
My heart, my very soul.
I find you in my thoughts every
Day—in my dreams each night.
I am held by a power that will
Neither take me in nor release me.
When I think I know you—
You surprise me with another face.
It's magical and wonderful and
My mind is consumed by you.

DOWNTOWN

I found myself downtown
    The other day. I wandered aimlessly
Down sidewalks thinking I'd find a
Window that would catch my eye—
    When I thought I saw you!
My heartbeat quickened and
    I followed you for a block—
Then I lost sight of you in the
    Noon day crowd.
I panicked and turned at the
    Corner catching a glimpse
Of you going into Macy's—so
    I followed.
As I went through the revolving
Door, I realized that Macy's
    Had closed years ago
And a remodeled office building
Had taken its place.
You were also gone—because
    You were never there.
My mind and focus left when
    You left.
I am alone now and
    Desperate to find you.
I need my sanity back
    And you hold the key.

PROMISE

Today, the drive took
    Us past fields of corn
        And beans.

Lush and green like love
    Or a new beginning—
        A fresh start.

Why do those days
    Seem to fly by
        And the dark days linger?

Why when you look at me
    Does the day seem
        Full of promise?

Why do I still find
    Myself alone
        At days end?

I don't seem to have any answers
    Only questions
        And solitary nights.

DOORWAYS

People don't notice vacant doorways,
Abandoned buildings, until they tear
Them down. But birds do. Yesterday
I saw a proud family who made its
Home over an unused door sill.
No one has disturbed them for a long
Time—long enough to build a nest
And raise a family. When did the going
In and coming out cease? When did
The structure die? When did we give up
On it? Why did we leave it without
Purpose? I ask these questions about
That lovely old building because I
Ask it of our love.

PAGES OF MY MIND

I find myself turning the pages
    Of my mind
And each page fills with the
    Memory of you.
Every day memories—special
    Memories.
But as I recall each day,
I discover all my memories
Of you were special.
The way you brushed your
Hair, put makeup on, and
So many of the mundane
Things we do each day.
I fill those pages with them all
Because they were all precious.
My mistake was taking them for
    Granted.
And now ... they are all I have.
All I cling too.
And so, as I sit alone and reflect,
I fill each page
One by one
    With memories
        Of you.

ALWAYS THERE

There are times when we are
　　Apart.
Traveling places without you.
But no matter where I lay
　　My head at night ...
　　　　You are with me.
The smell of your hair as your
　　Head lays on my shoulder;
You're quiet breathing,
　　Your hand on my chest,
　　　　Your gentle touch.
I am never without you.
　　Never alone.
When I close my eyes,
　　You are always there.
　　　　Always ...

THE WOMAN

Isn't it strange how life attacks emotions?
Yesterday, just casual friends exchanging courtesies.
Today, something much deeper.
It's difficult to discern when a year or two
Of friendship turned into something so beautiful.
Appearances haven't changed but the emotional
Involvement is quite intense now.
One day a friend, the next ...
It seems that I just noticed the woman in you.
Warm, caring, sensitive.
Needing the quiet reassurance that a man can give.
Sensing the longings that I find we share.
The secret desires; the unspoken thoughts
Read between the spoken words and daily niceties.
The innuendos and tenseness when we meet.
The sharing of private jokes when
In the company of others.
Yet knowing these dreams will go unfulfilled
Adds to the frustration, the pain, the heartache.
   Friends who want to be lovers.
   Lovers who want to be friends.
   Partners who want to be both but seldom are.
   So, we'll remain close without sharing.
   Friends without touching.
   Lovers within the bounds of our dreams.

WHISPERS

If I whispered your name
   Would you hear me?
Would you feel my soul
   Calling to yours?
Through these nights
   Of deep desperation,
All my days with no you
   And no sunshine.
Through the night with
   No moon and no stars;
Fate leads me to believe
   I'm alone, Dear
   Till you are back in my arms.

IDLE CHATTER

I'm not given to idle chatter—
Not in a bar sipping Port with friends;
Not when we are alone and I just want to look at you
Or hold your hand—see the love in your eyes.
Maybe just to watch you move in the silence.

Love is not something you suddenly put on
Like a winter coat to keep you warm.
Not even if it has a fur collar.

But rather, our love grew like a small child.
Rapidly at first and then a comfortable pace.
And then we settled in for a long trip that has no end.

And we gaze at the world together.
Eyes, hearts, minds and bodies becoming one.
Sometimes the lonely one but mostly
It's precious and wonderful—
Like you.

DREAMER

I was like you once.
    A young dreamer.
Reaching for adventure, building a career,
Being polite when I was supposed to be,
Trying to love and be loved.
But I'm older now and a whole lot more
Selfish with myself and my feelings.
I don't want to share me with just anyone—
    Not any longer.
I've given up on plastic and competing.
    Until you, perhaps.
You must understand that I haven't
Traveled uncharted waters in so many years.
And so it makes answering the simple
Questions very difficult. You're asking a
Withered flower to bloom again;
For sunrises and sunsets;
Dreams and daisies;
Loving and living.
I thought they'd all been used up—
    Until you.
I want desperately to believe you.
If only you knew. Because if I open
My eyes again—my heart, my soul,
And it all disappears—I don't think
I could bear the pain.
So give me just a little time to sort
Through memories and test the waters.

NOTHING LASTS FOREVER

Nothing lasts forever.
Nothing is here to stay.
The intimacies of a moment
Are forgotten in a day.

New fields we find;
Blue skies turn gray.
Nothing lasts forever
Nothing is here to stay.

FRIENDS AND LOVERS

I've watched them come and go.
The friends, the couples, the lovers.
As sure as the ebb and flow of the tide.
Only staying for a while—but eventually
To drift apart. To leave broken hearts
And dreams and sometimes lives.
Sometimes staying longer than the tide
Upon the sand—but leaving just as
Surely. To go out once again and
Try to capture new love.

DAWN HAS COME

Dawn has come and with it
The loneliness that comes
With waking alone. So long are
The nights; so empty the days.
Wandering aimlessly amid the
Noise and confusion. Coming
Home to empty rooms and faceless
Walls. Since you left, life
Has been a vacuum. Thoughts
Echoing in my mind—thoughts
Of you. Perhaps if I would
Have told you how I felt—
But it's too late now. As
Hopeless as reaching back to
Yesterday.

TOGETHER

Some day soon
   We will start
      Chasing dreams together.
No longer solitary.
   Staring at walls
      And hoping.
But together—
   One heart,
   One mind,
   One love.
Sharing dreams and sunrises
   And especially sunsets.

THE BRIDGE

Many times we stood and watched
The freight trains come and go.
From the bridge just down the street
In summer winds and winter snow.

It did not seem to matter then
Our comfort or the time;
Only that we heard the sound
Of lonely whistles whine.

We knew we'd be together soon
Our lives would be entwined.
So from the bridge we pledged our love;
Seems long ago... those times.

INTO THE WIND

Whether tangled branches
    Or tousled hair, no matter.
It just shows an uncluttered time
    When we walked straight into the wind
        Without fear or care.
We only have life to lose and that's not really
    Ours anyway.
Abandonment is what makes you beautiful.
It erases all the lines of age.
    Recaptures a moment we lived so long ago.
Are you holding my hand?
I can't feel you!
    From here on out, you'll have to go alone.
    But always walk straight into the wind—
    For me.

REMEMBERING

Every time I see lovers
   Holding hands
     And smiling,
Or stealing a casual kiss
   And laughing—
It hurts.
Now gone many days and
Many miles, I reach into
My memories to those precious
Few moments we spent together.
Remembering your smiles,
   Your laughs,
     Your touch.
Remembering—and holding on—
Until you return.

FOR YOU

For you,
    A tender kiss—
        For hours that turn into days.
        For days that turn into weeks.
        And weeks that turn into months.
For you,
    A gentle touch—
        For nights that never end,
        Lonely nights
        And empty pillows.
For you,
    All my love—
        To erase the empty days
        And lonely nights.
        And give you comfort.
For you,
    All of me—
        Forever
        With no turning back.

LEAVING

Knowing that you're leaving is like
Knowing someone is going to die!
It's something I can't change;
Much like the ache inside. At least
In going there is a counterpart—a
Chance of returning. Though my secret
Fear is that you'll find the grass
Greener elsewhere—without me.
You're young enough to recover, but
Being older, I haven't taken a
Chance in years. And my longing for
You scares me. And so now that
My defenses are down and my feelings
Exposed because I've been honest
With you—
Please be gentle.

SOMETIMES

Sometimes the absence of words
Say more than words could
Ever express. The look in your
Eyes; your gentle touch; your
Closeness; your embrace. Give
Your body to the passion of
Your mind. Let your heart
Express the flame in your soul.
Come with me and explore the
Heights and depths of love. Of
Passion that is ours to share.
Of love that has yet to be lived.

JOURNEY ALONE

If I could only stop thinking about
You, but your memory haunts me—
Is with me each waking hour—each
Dream filled night until I want to
Cry out. Can a feeling be so
Overpowering? And is it not
Shared? It seemed I've traveled
So many useless miles. So many
Miles filled with emptiness—
Secret longings—that even my
Memories are not fulfilling. I
Can start over, but we can't.
All I know is that I must
Journey alone.

THE HOPE OF LOVE

We must kiss—if only in our dreams.
We must touch—if only in the passing
Of our lives.
I'd know you if we met
But we haven't yet; and in my grasp
You are as gossamer.
Soft and fleeting, unable to be touched.
It seems that all I ever catch is
Just a glimpse.
Just enough to make my heart beat
A little faster.
Just enough to raise my hopes.
We get near enough, but not close enough,
To touch. Come to me—just once.
Once in this lifetime might be enough.
You can't run forever.
Stay out of my reach …
Dreams are more powerful than that.
And if I don't believe that,
I could not live another day.
Or would I want to.
So fleeting is a lifetime,
Yet all I ask is a moment—a touch—
A gentle kiss—the hope of love.

A Tear for Love

Tonight—more rain and more loneliness.
It's hard to believe
But when the sun comes up tomorrow
You will have gone—many miles—away.
Tonight I know sleeplessness;
The sound of the clock at three A.M.;
The dripping downspout;
The sound of silent tears upon my pillow.
How should I act as I watch my
    Life walk out the door?
I don't have the answer.
I just feel my life falling apart.
A good-bye kiss just doesn't cover it.
Not with the way we feel about each other.
All this emotion and never to have
Spent an evening alone—a private moment—
A night in each other's arms.
And so the ache I call a heart,
The emptiness I call a soul,
Will wander aimlessly until your return.
I know you will—by God you must!
And so tonight, I cried a tear for love.

Solitary Man

I am a solitary man.
But it doesn't mean I
Love you less. Perhaps
Just that I don't tell
You as often. But I do
Love you. I can't begin
To count the endless hours
I've watched you in your
Sleep. My silent tears
Absorbed by my pillow.
You—my only passion.
I hope you understand.
I could not bear to be
Without you.

THE POET

You shouldn't say a line
   You do not mean ...
You shouldn't think a line
   And not say it.
Because I will know!

I am the poet—the one
   Who sees your talk and
     Dreams
In surreal time and space;
And wanders through the
   Ethers ...
      Watching ...
        Listening ...
          Waiting ...
For that solitary moment
When what you do or do not say
   Will be written for all to
     See.

Put on pages,
Put in books,
Put on shelves.
   Waiting ...
     To expose your
Innermost longings for all to
   See.

Lyn Beyer was born and raised in St. Louis, Missouri. He graduated from the University of Missouri with a degree in Management. In his formative years, he played sports and read poetry at night under the covers with a flashlight because he was supposed to be sleeping. He has raised a family, lost a wife to cancer, and remarried. Poetry taught him to dream and that continues to this day. He is not ready to slow down or stop dreaming. His imagination and experience lead him forward.

www.ingramcontent.com/pod-product-compliance
Lightning Source LLC
Chambersburg PA
CBHW021347090426
42742CB00008B/770